POCKET-BOOK OF AFFIRMATIONS

time for joy

daily journal

By Ruth Fishel

Illustrations by Bonny Lowell

Health Communications, Inc.
Deerfield Beach, Florida

Ruth Fishel, M.Ed., C.A.C, is the co-founder and from 1974-1988 was co-director of Serenity, Inc., a multifaceted residential and out-patient treatment program for chemically dependent women and their families. She now teaches, writes and presents workshops and retreats throughout the country, helping people in all types of recovery to become whole and healthy, using the tools of meditation, affirmations and visualizations.

She is the author of *The Journey Within: A Spiritual Path To Recovery*, *Learning To Live In The Now: 6 Week Personal Plan to Recovery*, *Time For Joy*, a daily meditation and affirmations book, and booklets *From Medication To Meditation*, *21 Day Affirmations* and *A Pocket Full Of Love And Peace*.

Bonny Lowell is an illustrator of books and greeting cards, living and working in Massachusetts.

©1990 Ruth Fishel

ISBN 1-55874-063-5

Published by: Health Communications, Inc.
            3201 S.W. 15th Street
            Deerfield Beach, FL 33442

Today I am on my spiritual path to recovery.

_____

_____

_____

_____

_____

_____

January 1

I am beginning to trust myself. I am beginning to discover that I am okay.

January 2

I am discovering who I am with joy today.

January 3

*T*oday it is time to stop all my struggling and searching. It is time to be still. It is time to experience
peace. It is time
to find joy.

_____

_____

_____

_____

_____

_____

January 4

*T*oday I am willing to let go and let God work in my life. I am getting my self-will out of the way.

January 5

Even when I have doubt, I know that a power greater than myself is guiding me on my path today.

January 6

I am worthy of
positive changes
today!

January 7

I do not need to know anything about this day beyond this moment. This moment is perfect . . . just as it is and I can handle anything in this moment. My Higher Power gives me all the strength I need today to handle whatever comes up in this moment.

_____

_____

_____

_____

_____

_____

_____

January 8

I dare listen to my inner *voice with a new trust today!*

_____

_____

_____

_____

_____

_____

_____

January 9

*T*oday I am trusting the urge to move ahead . . . to grow . . . to risk new directions.

_____

_____

_____

_____

_____

_____

_____

January 10

I am listening to the voice of truth and love today.

January 11

Today I am willing to let go of all my fear so that I can find out what is real in my life. I will take whatever comes without judgment. I am ready to release all my resistance and struggle so that I can find the good and truth inside me.

_____

_____

_____

_____

_____

_____

January 12

"There are days when I doubt . . . myself . . . others . . . God. All I have to do when these feelings overwhelm me is to affirm myself and know all is okay. It is all right to doubt. Trust will replace doubt if I am patient and easy on myself."

Maureen Lydon

Trust will replace doubt if I am patient . . .

_____

_____

_____

_____

_____

_____

_____

January 13

I am clearing out old confusion and doubt so that I can see the miracles today.

January 14

I celebrate myself today. I am alive. I am growing, I am willing to do all I am able to do to be the best of who I am.

January 15

joy!

Today I take the time to be with me and find peace and love and truth. It is mine if I just stop. It is mine if I just think the thoughts I want to feel.

_____

_____

_____

_____

_____

_____

January 16

Today I am not afraid of the silence. I find peace in this silence and I am able to listen to God's will for me.

January 17

"Most people fail because they do not wake and see when they stand at the fork in the road and have to decide."

Erich Fromm

My Higher Power guides me today. I can move forward with the faith and trust that I am being lovingly led along the way, a step at a time, a day at a time.

January 18

My Higher Power guides me in making all healthy and positive decisions today.

_____

_____

_____

_____

_____

_____

_____

January 19

I choose to live
in the light of
my truth today.

January 20

I deserve wonderful things to happen in my life today.

_____

_____

_____

_____

_____

_____

_____

January 21

*A*s I take the
time to let
my stress go today
I will be filled
with love and joy
and peace. I will
be aware of these
feelings thoughout
my day and share
them with others.

January 22

I let God guide me in my recovery today, knowing that all decisions that come from good and love will bring me joy.

_____

_____

_____

_____

_____

_____

_____

January 23

Today I will accept all of me just as I am. I will put aside all judgments and I will rejoice in the miracle of my uniqueness.

_____

_____

_____

_____

_____

_____

_____

January 24

As I go about my day I trust all my decisions to my positive inner guide. Nothing from the past will block me or hold me back. Today is mine to use for growth and recovery. I love myself today.

January 25

this is fun!

Nothing can stop
me from growing
today.

January 26

As I stop today and take the time to be still, I become in touch with my Higher Power. I feel myself filling with love and peace as I relax and let go of the stress in my day.

_____

_____

_____

_____

_____

_____

_____

January 27

*A*s I continue to grow on my spiritual path to recovery, I bask in the miracles of transformation and healing that are taking place in my life today.

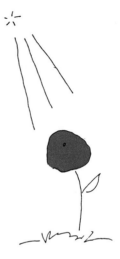

_____

_____

_____

_____

_____

_____

January 28

*T*oday I will treat myself to quiet time. Today I will be gentle with myself as I let myself do nothing but be who I am. Today I will value what I think.

January 29

*T*oday I give myself permission to take the quiet time I need to meditate and to improve my conscious contact with God.

January 30

I will take the time I need for me today to be quiet and listen to my Higher Power as I gently make new discoveries and gain new wisdom.

January 31

*"Recovery is a path . . .
not a sudden landing."*
Sandra Bierig

I know that one step at a time I am making progress today. I am grateful for all my growth even if it is not always very obvious.

_____

_____

_____

_____

_____

_____

February 1

As I gently pull back each layer that has been blocking me from being the best of who I am, I dare look a bit further and then a bit further yet. I know that I am not alone on this path and God is guiding me every inch of the way.

February 2

I am no longer a victim of my past. I am free to move in new directions today. I am at choice in my life.

PaST

_____

_____

_____

_____

_____

_____

_____

February 3

*T*oday I dare look within to see what is keeping me stuck. I know I cannot change unless I know what there is to change. I feel energized and empowered to move forward.

_____

_____

_____

_____

_____

_____

_____

February 4

Today I dare to walk a new path where comfort and security are not my goals. I dare to reach out to my fellow human beings and become part of a society whose aim is peace and love and joy and recovery.

February 5

I am slowly finding new strength within me as I begin to trust my inner voice. I dare listen and take new risks as I follow my inner path.

February 6

I feel my entire body unwinding and relaxing as I give up my resistance and struggle. Today I accept life as it comes and learn to flow with it with peace.

joy

February 7

"*A*m I willing to unlearn my tensions?"

Amy Dean

_____

_____

_____

_____

_____

_____

_____

February 8

Today I have the courage to follow my own inner voice that I hear in prayer and meditation. Today I dare to be true to myself and my own needs, whether anyone agrees with me or not.

February 9

Today I will look inside for my answers. Today I will trust my instincts and my connection to my Higher Power.

February 10

*E*ven in moments of doubt I know
that my Higher Power is guiding
me on my path today.

_____

_____

_____

_____

_____

_____

February 11

Today I am willing to let go of all the negative tapes that I hear that block me from my truth. And as I let go, I trust and follow the energy that leads me to peace and joy.

_____

_____

_____

_____

_____

_____

February 12

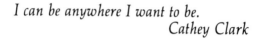

I can be anywhere I want to be.
                        Cathey Clark

_____

_____

_____

_____

_____

_____

_____

February 13

I am beginning to actually feel the energy of love I have inside. My entire being is in the process of being transformed with love.

February 14

i like me!

Today I will 'act as if' I am worth loving. I will begin by telling myself that I am worthy of loving myself. I will acknowledge all the good and lovable things about me. I will 'act as if' until I know that it is true.

February 15

peace

relaxation

*P*eace and relaxa-
tion flow through
me with every
breath I take.

_____

_____

_____

_____

_____

_____

_____

February 16

*E*ven in moments of doubt, I know that my
Higher Power is guiding me on my path
today.

_____

_____

_____

_____

_____

_____

_____

February 17

> "*Today I am establishing rapport with myself.*"
>
> *Peter Vegso*

_____

_____

_____

_____

_____

_____

_____

February 18

Today I know that I am doing the best I can and will be gentle with myself. I will watch what comes without struggle and will accept what is and adjust myself to it, rather than wanting it to be different than it is.

_____

_____

_____

_____

_____

_____

_____

February 19

I know that I am be-
ing led along a path
of healing today. As I
become more and more
open to spirituality and
recovery, my path be-
comes brighter and
clearer every day.

find a star

February 20

your strength within you!

*I*t is exciting to know that
I have all the strength I
need today to do all that is
good and right in my life.

February 21

God is guiding me on my path to self-sufficiency and independence today. As I become willing to let go of my feelings of inferiority and weakness, my Higher Power gives me all the strength that I need for all that comes up for me today.

_____

_____

_____

_____

_____

_____

February 22

*T*oday I have the courage to own my own unhappiness, daring to look within to discover its source. Today, I treat myself as a friend with gentleness and acceptance.

February 23

I am growing in my ability to trust what feels good and right. Today I can look within and wait until I know with my heart.

love

February 24

I will give myself the gift of time today to be quiet and hear with my heart. I will go to my special place inside where I really live in love and in joy and carry those feelings with me throughout the day.

_____

_____

_____

_____

_____

_____

February 25 ·

It feels so safe to know that there is always a special place within me where I can feel peace.

February 26

*T*oday I will trust myself when something does not feel smooth and flowing. I will begin to look around for alternatives to anything that feels rough and irritating.

February 27

"God does not require from novices prayer completely free from distractions. Do not despond when your thought is distracted, but remain calm, and unceasingly restore your mind to itself."

St. John of the Ladder

I am accepting what comes up today without reaction and judgment. I see simply that what is there is there, and by this simple acceptance of the truth I can relax and flow with the day.

_____

_____

_____

_____

_____

_____

_____

February 28

Today I will feel good about myself and accept myself just the way I am. I am open and ready to discover all the miracles of this day.

little miracles are everywhere ✩

_____

_____

_____

_____

_____

_____

March 1

*T*oday I am letting go of all energy that is resisting the truth about me. This energy is being replaced with positive and loving energy and I am accepting that I am okay just the way I am. I am now open to see the miracles of love in my life.

March 2

Today I will stop and ask how important is it? When I find myself defending or trying to prove my point. I am in the process of learning to trust my own truth. When it feels right inside, I am seeing that it is all I need.

_____

_____

_____

_____

_____

_____

_____

March 3

Where I am at this moment is perfect. My past is my friend today as I take the lessons that I can learn from it and say thank you. Everything that has brought me to this moment is a gift and I am a stronger and wiser person because of it.

my past

March 4

*T*oday I will accept what I have, and what I
am, and what I see in this moment. I will be
fully alive in this
moment and feel
the joy of knowing
that it is all that
there is right now.

_____

_____

_____

_____

_____

_____

March 5

I am learning to trust my instincts and move away from unpleasant and stressful people, places and things. I no longer have to stay in situations that bring me unhappiness and pain. I am turning around today to see the joy.

March 6

I feel so good knowing that I am a power of example to future generations today as I walk on my new path of truth. I am making a difference not only in my own life but in the lives of those who follow me.

March 7

I trust all that comes up for me today. I now know there is no value in hiding the truth from myself. I choose today to know everything about me and I am excited about this new adventure.

March 8

Today I know that I am in charge of the quality of my life. I am growing in the ability to become aware of the thoughts that have been controlling me.

March 9

I am open and willing today to take a step forward in a new direction. I am no longer allowing myself to stay stuck by old thoughts and feelings. This new place is exciting and energizing.

_____

_____

_____

_____

_____

_____

_____

March 10

Today I continue to let go of all thoughts that have been pulling me out of the present and bringing me to the past and future. I am becoming more and more open to let the power of good and love enter my life.

_____

_____

_____

_____

_____

_____

March 11

I can be centered and at peace inside when the world is going my way as well as when things are happening that are not my choice. I am learning to focus on this newly found inner peace, especially at times of confusion and stress.

_____

_____

_____

_____

_____

_____

March 12

"The need to grow, to change, to affect the world around us is part of God's plan for each of us. I will trust the urge. I will let it guide my steps."

Each Day A New Beginning

I have a purpose today. As I let go and let God, this purpose is becoming more and more clear. My heart is full of joy and love as I move more towards God's will for me.

_____

_____

_____

_____

_____

_____

_____

March 13

"To accept ourselves as we are means to value our imperfections as much as our perfections."

Sandra Bierig

I will value myself today both for my perfections and especially for my imperfections.

_____

_____

_____

_____

_____

_____

_____

March 14

"I have outgrown the need to suffer.
Al-Anon Expression

M y Higher Power guides me in directions that fill positive needs in my life today. I have grown to see that my true needs are love and peace and joy.

_____

_____

_____

_____

_____

_____

_____

March 15

*C*hoosing positive thoughts and making positive choices fill me with new strength, confidence and excitement. I can feel positive energy flow through me with every positive thought I choose.

March 16

*T*oday I know I have a right to be alive and happy and full of joy. Today I trust that I am where I am supposed to be, and am moving in the right direction.

_____

_____

_____

_____

_____

_____

March 17

Don't hide your light under a lampshade.

don't hide
it!

*T*oday I will be part of the main stream of life, letting people see me as I am. I will share what I have when it can be useful, looking for opportunities to give to others the best of who I am.

March 18

*T*oday I dare to openly express my needs and find healthy ways to get them met. I like feeling good today. I like myself today.

March 19

stuck!

I am becoming more open to look within me today for my solutions. I trust that I will find the right answers if I go quietly within and follow my inner guide.

_____

_____

_____

_____

_____

_____

March 20

*G*od is guiding me in peace and in calm today. I know that anything upsetting this feeling is not permanent and will pass. I no longer allow upsets to keep me from seeing the good in others.

_____

_____

_____

_____

_____

_____

_____

March 21

No matter how busy I am today, I will begin and end my day with quiet time. I look forward to that time when I stop all outward activity, rest and look within for my peace and truth.

_____

_____

_____

_____

_____

_____

_____

March 22

Today I no longer struggle to find my answers alone. I welcome and am open to positive and healthy support wherever I find it.

March 23

I forgive myself and all others today.

March 24

*M*y Higher Power is with me in the sun as well as the rain, in pain as well as joy. As long as I know that I am protected and guided by the power of faith and love, I will remain centered and balanced through all of this day.

March 25

God gives me all the willingness I need today to sit quietly and listen.

⁙

March 26

I am good enough . . . just
the way I am!

_____

_____

_____

_____

_____

_____

_____

March 27

I am at choice today. I can watch my negative thoughts go by and replace them with positive thoughts of love and compassion.

March 28

_____

_____

_____

_____

_____

_____

_____

*G*od gives me all the strength and courage to accept whatever happens in my life today. It is so freeing to know that I am no longer a victim of people, places and things.

_____

_____

_____

_____

_____

_____

March 29

My Higher Power is guiding me with my positive attitude today. Negatives are no longer something I choose to live with. I feel positive strength pour through me as I release all negative thoughts.

_____

_____

_____

_____

_____

_____

March 30

With softness and gentleness I am turning around all negative thinking so that my mind is positive. It feels so good to be in charge of the world that I am creating for myself.

_____

_____

_____

_____

_____

_____

_____

March 31

I accept myself today and am grateful that I can grow from where I am. As I bring more and more love to myself, I continue to blossom and expand, growing to be the best of who I can be.

_____

_____

_____

_____

_____

_____

April 1

Today I wait in peace and rest in the knowledge that God is working for me while I am resting.

_____

_____

_____

_____

_____

_____

April 2

I am open to positive changes in my life today.

April 3

*T*oday I am hanging in no matter what. Even when my conscious mind wants to give up, I will reach for that healthy, loving part deep within me and with the help of prayer and meditation and the good people in my life, I will find a rainbow.

April 4

*T*oday I am open to all of who I am. As I bring my attention to all of me, without judgment, I grow in wisdom and freedom.

_____

_____

_____

_____

_____

_____

_____

April 5

Today I am breaking out of old patterns, rewriting old tapes and letting my life flow with love and joy.

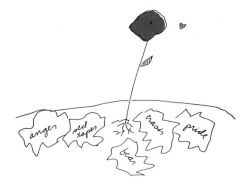

_____

_____

_____

_____

_____

_____

April 6

"If I lose my direction, I have to look for the North Star, and I go to the north. That does not mean that I expect to arrive at the North Star. I just want to go in that direction."

Thich Nhat Hanh

I am moving towards my goals today with just the right energy that I need. My progress will be perfect and I have the faith and trust that all the steps that I take along the way will become clear when that is necessary.

_____

_____

_____

_____

_____

April 7

*T*oday I can find peace within myself without needing the approval and agreement of others. Today I can love and respect people who do not always share in my view of the world.

_____

_____

_____

_____

_____

_____

April 8

"And could you keep your heart in wonder at the daily miracles of your life, your pain would not seem less wondrous than your joy."

Kahlil Gibran

My heart is open to all that happens in my life today. There is such joy at being alive and feeling everything with a full and open heart.

April 9

*I am so grateful for the guidance I have
received in my recovery.*

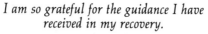

I am attracted to positive people and I attract positive people to me. Today I continue to seek and find people who are positive, healthy and nurturing.

_____

_____

_____

_____

_____

_____

April 10

*T*he more I let go of my own suffering and self-pity, I can see those around me with the eyes of love and compassion. I am becoming more aware of other peoples' pain and unhappiness today and I will reach out to them in loving ways that heal me while I am helping to heal them.

April 11

Today I know that everytime I inhale, I am breathing in powerful, healing energy. And everytime I exhale, I am letting go. I am letting go of all anxiety, all stress . . . all negativity that is standing in the way of my feeling good about myself.

April 12

*T*oday I have faith and perseverance to stay on my path and do what is necessary whether or not it gives me immediate results and gratification. I am letting go of my impatience, procrastination, fear and doubt. I trust that God knows the right time for the right results.

i have faith.

April 13

"When we refuse air, light and food, the body suffers. And when we turn away from meditation and prayer, we likewise deprive our minds, our emotions and our intuitions of vitally needed support. As the body can fail its purpose for lack of nourishment, so can the soul."
    Alcoholics Anonymous, World Service, Inc.

*T*oday I am growing in my awareness that my mind, body and spirit need exercise and nourishment. Through prayer and meditation, exercise and inspirational reading, I am developing a personal program for physical, mental and spiritual growth.

_____

_____

_____

_____

_____

April 14

I *will put aside all judgments and accept each and every situation with openness and trust today. Only then will I discover the joy that lies beyond my fear.*

my fears

joy

_____

_____

_____

_____

_____

_____

April 15

Today I picture myself flooded with the glow of a powerful bright light that is guiding me on my positive path of success and happiness.

April 16

I have been given gifts which will make me feel ful-filled only when I have used them for others as well as for myself. Keeping myself to myself is a waste of my ability to become truly whole.

I will open myself up to all the possibilities around me today, leaving my fear of change behind.

_____

_____

_____

_____

_____

_____

_____

April 17

Today I need to do nothing more than pray and meditate. I trust that all the energies of the universe are working in my behalf. I can sleep comfortably in the knowledge that God is working when I am not.

_____

_____

_____

_____

_____

_____

April 18

> "Learn to look at other human beings
> with the eyes of compassion."
> *Thich Nhat Hanh*

*I*f any negative feelings are triggered in me today, I will not act on my first impulse or desire. I will stop and get in touch with my breathing and my connections with the universe. I will take time to remember to see the other person's point of view.

_____

_____

_____

_____

_____

_____

April 19

I can handle anything that comes up today . . . even if it is only for a moment at a time.

_____

_____

_____

_____

_____

_____

April 20

"If healing is about being whole, then every expression of being wants acknowledgment, including the things I don't like."

Dianne M. Connelly

*I*t feels terrific letting go of perfection as my goal. As I let go of my judgments, all parts of me come together and I feel complete.

April 21

"If you cannot be compassionate to yourself, you will not be able to be compassionate to others."

Thich Nhat Hanh

*T*oday I will be aware not to judge myself when I act "less than perfect". I am beginning to love myself just as I am and that feels so nice.

_____

_____

_____

_____

_____

_____

_____

April 22

*T*oday I can set my goals with the clear and confident knowledge that I can only do one

thing at a time and take one step at a time towards that goal. I do not need to wait until I reach that goal to be happy and satisfied. I am fulfilled with each step, knowing that is all I can do in each moment.

April 23

"When you understand, you cannot help but love. You cannot get angry. To develop understanding, you have to practice looking at all living beings with the eyes of compassion. When you understand, you love. And when you love, you naturally act in a way that can relieve the suffering of people."

Thich Nhat Hanh

Today I am practicing looking at all beings with the eyes of compassion.

April 24

*P*ositive energy attracts positive energy. Today my Higher Power continues to guide my growth so that I am more and more open. I am becoming free and unblocked and am attracting all that is good and right in my life.

_____

_____

_____

_____

_____

_____

_____

April 25

Today I am open to all the powers of the universe. I am letting them work for me and carry me to my next step . . . JOY!

April 26

*T*oday I have the courage to face life as it is and make progress a part of my life. I am willing to take chances and grow and risk and feel what it means to be fully alive in the moment.

_____

_____

_____

_____

_____

_____

_____

April 27

It is exciting to know that my thoughts and my actions in the present moment condition the next moment. I am responsible for my future. Today I am bringing awareness to my self-talk, and replacing all negative thoughts with positive thoughts as soon as they appear on my mindscape.

April 28

With every breath that I take,
healing is taking place
whether I am aware of it or not.
I relax safely in the knowledge that
positive, healing energy is working
in my life today.
I am being renewed and refreshed and energized.

April 29

*A*s I start this day with quiet meditation, I feel myself becoming still and at peace. At any time during the day I can bring my mind back to this moment. I will bring my attention and awareness back to the peace that I have when I am with my breath and I know that my breath is with me at all times, whether I remember it or not.

April 30

When I look within, I find I have all that I need. It feels wonderful to discover that I already am the beautiful person that I would like to be.

_____

_____

_____

_____

_____

_____

May 1

Today I am open to making small changes in my life that lead me, a step at a time, on my spiritual path to recovery. I have faith in the guidance that I am receiving. I trust that I will know intuitively when the time for these changes is right.

_____

_____

_____

_____

_____

_____

_____

May 2

my beautiful now!

I t is beautiful to know that I am the creator of the way I think and feel today, that I can choose my now. Today I choose to feel joy and I will do all that I have to do to make that possible.

_____

_____

_____

_____

_____

_____

May 3

*T*oday I choose to think positive and loving thoughts. I know that if I do this I will feel loving and positive and create a positive and loving world for myself and those around me.

May 4

*T*oday I will let my Higher Power handle my worry so that I can be free. I choose to be alive in this moment and not blocked by the conversations that go on over and over in my head. I will stop trying to figure everything out and will trust that I will get the right answers at the right time.

May 5

Today I feel my entire body energized by my powerful, positive thoughts. I feel alive and full of joy as I feed myself with loving and positive energy.

_____

_____

_____

_____

_____

_____

May 6

Today I choose to accept life on its terms . . . all of them. I am open to all I see, hear, think and feel in the moment without resistance. I am open to being fully alive and enjoying the adventure.

May 7

I am letting go of all self-criticism today and changing all my judging thoughts to thoughts of love. I am becoming softer and more gentle and accepting of myself, making more space to feel love and joy.

_____

_____

_____

_____

_____

_____

May 8

Today I am letting a power greater than myself remove all my fear. I am now free to look within for my answers. I no longer bury myself with people, places and things.

May 9

"Lord make me an instrument of Thy peace . . ."
St. Francis of Assisi

Spiritual and emotional health are a natural result of being willing to look only for beauty in even the smallest and least powerful of the earth's creatures.

Today I will look for opportunities to continue to grow through seeing the beauty around me, and in me.

_____

_____

_____

_____

_____

_____

May 10

*T*oday my trust in the overall and the long run is deep within me and growing. When events and people do not act as I would like them to act, I reach deeper inside for my faith and let it comfort me.

May 11

When I place myself in the hands and heart of my Higher Power today, I know that I will get my needs met. Only then do I trust that I will come from good and love, keeping the good of others in my mind and heart.

_____

_____

_____

_____

_____

_____

May 12

Today I will wait in quiet and faith for a clear answer before making any decisions. Today I feel secure, trusting that my instincts are guiding me on every step on my path.

May 13

"In the coming decades, the most important determinants of health and longevity will be the personal choices made by each individual."

Journal of the American Medical Association

I have all the power I need today to say no to negative choices.

_____

_____

_____

_____

_____

_____

May 14

It is exciting to know that the more I listen to the chattering that goes on in my mind, the quicker I can identify the blocks to my positive and creative energy. Today I release all negativity so that I can be fully alive in the moment.

May 15

I begin my day with quiet time, finding peace and serenity in my meditation. I carry those feelings with me wherever I am. If anything happens to disturb this peace, I can stop and spend a few minutes with my breath and regain my serenity.

May 16

Today I know that with every in-breath, I am breathing in powerful, healing, energy. And with every out-breath I am letting go. I am letting go of all anxiety, all stress . . . all negativity that is standing in the way of my feeling good about myself.

May 17

*T*oday I look beyond the immediate moment of satisfaction and decide what is good for me in the larger picture of my life. Today I have faith and patience and can wait to make loving and positive choices.

_____

_____

_____

_____

_____

_____

May 18

I love the person that I am becoming!

_____

_____

_____

_____

_____

_____

May 19

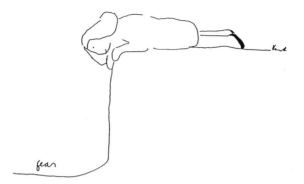

*T*oday I will look at all my fears in a new light. I can now see them as a result of my thinking and will turn over all my fearful thoughts to my Higher Power. Fear no longer owns me or is a threat to my day.

_____

_____

_____

_____

_____

_____

May 20

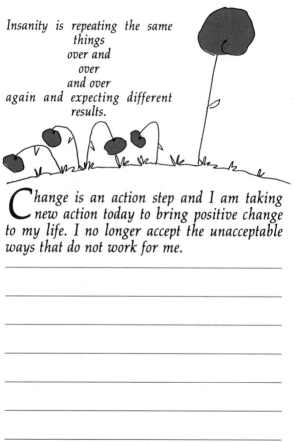

Insanity is repeating the same
things
over and
over
and over
again and expecting different
results.

*C*hange *is an action step and I am taking*
new action today to bring positive change
to my life. I no longer accept the unacceptable
ways that do not work for me.

May 21

Today I choose to
feel love in this
moment. Today I
choose to let love fill
my day and bring joy.

May 22

THIS MOMENT

I do not need to know anything about this day beyond this moment. This moment is perfect . . . just as it is and I can handle anything in this moment. My Higher Power gives me all the strength I need today to handle whatever comes up in this moment.

_____

_____

_____

_____

_____

_____

_____

May 23

Today I dare to believe in the beauty of love. Today I trust that I am being led to love and my day will be full of love.

_____

_____

_____

_____

_____

_____

_____

May 24

I celebrate myself today. I am alive. I am growing. I am willing to do all I am able to do to be the best of who I am.

_____

_____

_____

_____

_____

_____

_____

May 25

*T*oday I know that I am being guided and protected by a power greater than myself. I look forward to the unknown around the next bend in the road, the adventure over the next hill.

May 26

I will take all the time I need to keep in touch with my Higher Power today. Meditation slows me down and brings me peace at all moments I choose.

May 27

Nothing can stop me from feeling wonderful today. I am filled with all the wonder and splendor of the universe and I pass this on to everyone I meet.

May 28

*T*oday I will be gentle with myself as I meditate and look within. I will look at my inner self lovingly and without judgment as I find the blocks that have kept me stuck.

May 29

I am putting a large stop sign to all my negative self-talk today.

_____

_____

_____

_____

_____

_____

_____

May 30

Today I continue to remove any barriers that keep me from being fully who I am in this universe. As I continue to trust my inner guidance, I receive all the inspiration I need to grow in courage and faith and love.

May 31

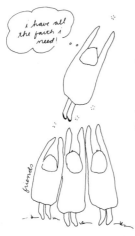

*T*oday I know that my Higher Power gives me all the strength that I need to move forward. I can feel this strength growing within me as I dare to take one new step at a time.

_____

_____

_____

_____

_____

_____

_____

June 1

"Today I know that I cannot control the ocean tides. I can only go with the flow. Today I can learn how to float to the top and let myself be carried buoyantly, joyously through life. When I struggle and try to organize the Atlantic to my specifications, I sink. If I flail and thrash, and growl and grumble, I go under. But if I let go and float, I am borne aloft."

Marie Stilkind

*T*oday I choose to go with the flow.

_____

_____

_____

_____

_____

_____

June 2

This morning and evening I will take the time that I need to be still and hear God's will for me. This thought alone brings me peace. This commitment brings me serenity.

_____

_____

_____

_____

_____

_____

_____

June 3

This day is full of miracles. They are right in front of me on my path. Today I have the courage to let go of all that is holding me back so that I step forward and experience each miracle waiting for me.

_____

_____

_____

_____

_____

_____

_____

June 4

*P*eace and relaxation flow through me with every breath that I take. I am complete in this moment.

_____

_____

_____

_____

_____

_____

June 5

I know that I cannot be hurt by people if I consistently look for their best. Today I continue to search out the best in all my relationships, looking for something I can love in everyone.

_____

_____

_____

_____

_____

_____

_____

June 6

*T*oday I am willing to experience all my feelings, without hiding or running away. I am feeling alive in all moments and I am living this day to the fullest.

_____

_____

_____

_____

_____

_____

_____

June 7

Today I do all the footwork I can to make my life work. I trust the results to God and know that they will be just what is good and right for me.

_____

_____

_____

_____

_____

_____

June 8

I am discovering all the love I have
within me.

_____

_____

_____

_____

_____

_____

June 9

Today my heart brings me to new places of giving and sharing that I have not yet experienced. I am a friend today and get great satisfaction when I put the needs of others first because I want to, not because I think I have to do so.

_____

_____

_____

_____

_____

_____

June 10

Today I have the courage to look without fear at what needs to be changed in my life.

June 11

*T*oday I will honor
my own values,
and be open to change
as a result of growth.

June 12

I am open to experience my connection with God and all the people I meet on my path today. There is new joy each time I realize our sameness rather than our separateness.

_____

_____

_____

_____

_____

_____

_____

June 13

It is exciting to know that I am in charge of my life today. God gives me all the faith and courage I need to be present and aware in each moment and the wisdom to see what needs to be done.

past   now   future

_____

_____

_____

_____

_____

_____

June 14

Today I will stop and remember all the times I gave lovingly of myself and know that these were my successes. I am a very rich person when I understand that the moments coming from love cannot be measured on any scale. They are priceless.

June 15

"Scientists tell us that our body is constantly rebuilding and curing itself. When the body is fed the mental picture of wholeness, it builds its cells according to that picture, whereas when fed thoughts of incurability, the body builds the cells according to that mental picture."
Catherine Ponder

*T*oday I choose to see myself well and wholesome. Today I put all my energy into positive thoughts, knowing that my body is healthy and strong.

June 16

I am learning new ways to deal with all that comes up in my life today. I am letting go of all negative ways of dealing with stress and anxiety that are harmful to my mind and body.

letting go

June 17

"Some days I realize that many things can fragment my life. Then I can forget the focus and find I am agitated and nervous. Now I know that these feelings are a signal to sit and rest. During the quiet I can go inside and calm and restrengthen myself."

Eileen White

*T*oday my body guides me to refocus, and God heals me deep within as I again become strong and free.

June 18

Today I will look honestly at what is real without denial and judgment. I accept my reality without struggle and this gives me all the energy I need to deal with what needs to be done.

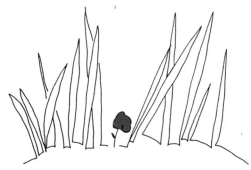

June 19

*M*y past experiences no longer take up room and live in my mind and body. I am free to live in today.

June 20

*I*t feels so good to know that no matter what is going on today, I have the faith to know that my Higher Power is guiding and supporting me.

June 21

*T*oday I know that I am not the best or the worst. I am just me. God is guiding me to become the best me I can be and that is very exciting.

"i love you" God

_____

_____

_____

_____

_____

June 22

*T*oday I am learning to release my stress and anxiety in positive and healthy ways. My body is becoming free from all negative experiences. My past no longer lives in my body.

_____

_____

_____

_____

_____

_____

June 23

I love me because of all that I am, not just a part of me. I fully accept myself just as I am today and that feels so good.

_____

_____

_____

_____

_____

_____

June 24

*T*oday I sit quietly in prayer and meditation so that I can hear God's will for me. I know I am being guided in this very moment.

_____

_____

_____

_____

_____

_____

_____

June 25

Today I am willing to let go of all the resentments I am holding. My now is so much more important than the burden that I have been carrying from the past.

now

_____

_____

_____

_____

_____

_____

June 26

*T*oday I am learning to be gentle with myself. Today I can look in the mirror and smile and know that I am OK, just as I am. I am treating myself softly today.

_____

_____

_____

_____

_____

_____

_____

June 27

"All problems fade out in proportion as you develop the ability to be quiet, to behold and to witness divine harmony unfold . . ."

Joel S. Goldsmith

release the energy!

M y quiet sitting meditation time helps me to develop new quiet times during the rest of the day. Today I can look at any problem I have and release its energy so that I can be free to allow harmony to unfold.

_____

_____

_____

_____

_____

_____

_____

June 28

Today I am becoming more and more aware that I can choose how I feel in the moment. Today I choose to let go of thoughts that are negative and destructive. Today I choose to feel good.

June 29

POSITIVE THOUGHTS!

*T*oday I will listen to the messages that go on in my head and decide for myself if they are healthy. Today I will choose to follow positive messages I tell myself, or create new messages that are positive and healthy.

_____

_____

_____

_____

_____

_____

June 30

Today I trust my instincts. Today I trust that I will know at the right time the right answer. Today I have the faith to know that God guides me in my choices.

July 1

I am accepting myself just as I am, imperfections and all. I am not striving to be perfect today. I only want to grow, to change, to become more and more open and to let God and love be in charge of my life.

_____

_____

_____

_____

_____

_____

_____

July 2

Today I can search my own heart and discover whether my intentions are for positive or constructive reasons. Today I can trust that when I come from good and love, I am making the right choices.

July 3

*T*oday I will find someone less fortunate than I and give her what I can. Today I will let go of my own troubles and self-pity by finding someone I can help.

_____

_____

_____

_____

_____

_____

_____

July 4

"There, but for the grace of God go I."

I am grateful!

I am very grateful to be exactly where I am today. I do not need to be a victim of my past or controlled by circumstances. I am in recovery today and it feels wonderful.

_____

_____

_____

_____

_____

_____

July 5

*I*t is a great relief to know that all I have to do is turn to the twelve steps of recovery and help is with me. Today I am given all the tools that I need and am so grateful that I no longer have to struggle alone.

_____

_____

_____

_____

_____

_____

July 6

*T*oday I let go totally and give God
space to do his work.

_____

_____

_____

_____

_____

_____

_____

July 7

When I find myself slipping back to 'what ifs' and 'if onlys', I will pause for a moment and remember to have gratitude for what is. I am grateful today and that gives me loving energy.

_____

_____

_____

_____

_____

_____

_____

July 8

*T*oday I am learning to stop judging and comparing so that I can be with what is. I am learning to accept what is and be with what is as it is without the struggle of trying to decide whether it is right or wrong.

_____

_____

_____

_____

_____

_____

July 9

Today I will share my strength, hope and experience with someone still in pain. I will serve as a power of example to someone who is willing to let go of his suffering.

i remembers!

_____

_____

_____

_____

_____

_____

July 10

There are times when you must "march to the beat of a different drummer, no matter how distant."

Today I look within to find my truth. I ask a power greater than myself to guide me and show me the way and all I have to do is follow. It is that simple.

July 11

I am at choice today. I accept the responsibility of my life with a new sense of maturity, confidence and even excitement.

_____

_____

_____

_____

_____

_____

_____

July 12

"There is no winter harsh enough to withhold the promise of spring."

Karen Kaiser Clarke

I can go through anything a day at a time, a moment at a time, with the faith and the knowledge that my Higher Power is guiding me to peace and security.

_____

_____

_____

_____

_____

_____

July 13

*T*oday I know that if I am coming from good and love, then only good and love will happen. Today I know that what I give, I receive back.

July 14

*T*oday I choose to think positive. Today I let my thoughts lead the way to success and happiness.

July 15

Today I am willing to give away what I need for myself. I am willing to listen to someone else's problems. That way we will both see that we are traveling together on the same journey and are not alone.

July 16

*G*od gives me all the answers I need at the right time. Today I trust that it is okay not to know everything and that I will know when the time is right.

_____

_____

_____

_____

_____

_____

_____

July 17

*F*ears sometimes
still linger in my
mind. I can be okay
when that happens. I
can feel them through and
talk about them and go on in
spite of them, not letting myself
picture the worst, but seeing the
results in a positive light.

July 18

*T*oday I have faith that I am being led to the answers that I need to learn. If I keep putting one foot in front of the other, I will always be in a safe place.

_____

_____

_____

_____

_____

_____

_____

July 19

*T*oday I am reaching out to those who love and support me. I am letting go of my ego and self-centeredness so that I can make space to take in love and support and ideas from others.

_____

_____

_____

_____

_____

_____

July 20

oday I am open to everyone who is on my path, whether I know her or not. Somewhere there will be someone who needs my help and I want to be there for him. My Higher Power will tell me what needs to be done.

July 21

*T*oday I am growing in my faith that I dare to look at what is really disturbing my serenity. Today I trust that by searching deep within for my own truth, I will discover the door to freedom and peace.

July 22

Today I will put aside all negative and destructive thoughts so that I can come from a place of love. Today I will let go of all blame and anger and resentments so that my heart and my mind will be open and free to feel love and give love.

July 23

Today I am going to spend more time looking for all the positive things about myself. Today I recognize myself and acknowledge myself as a terrific human being.

July 24

When I turn a problem over to my Higher Power today, I will let it go with the confidence that all is being handled for me. After I have done all my footwork, I know that the results will work out just as they are supposed to.

July 25

*T*oday I will allow myself to just be without judgment, without criticism. I will accept all that happens with love and gentleness.

July 26

Today I release all thoughts and feelings that cause me harm. I am learning to put all fears aside and come from a place of truth and love. The rewards of this freedom are far greater than the negative results of my fear.

_____

_____

_____

_____

_____

_____

_____

July 27

*I*t is exciting to know that I am at choice today and that my choices are limitless. I can choose exactly what I want to do to change how I am feeling.

_____

_____

_____

_____

_____

_____

_____

July 28

*T*oday I know
that I am being
guided and protected
in my path for
growth and freedom.
All the positive
energy in the uni-
verse is working for
my greatest good.
All I have to do is
put one foot in front
of the other.

July 29

just watch me grow! ♥

I am developing new and positive habits today.
I am putting all my energy into moving
forward and building a healthy life.

_____

_____

_____

_____

_____

_____

_____

July 30

*M*y heart is full of gratitude today. I am free today to experience this day fully and to follow my spiritual path. I have been given a new day to live, to grow, to give love and to feel love.

July 31

*T*oday I choose to forgive instead of holding onto resentments. Today I choose to let go of all feelings that block me from feeling love. Today I choose to see everyone with the eyes of love.

_____

_____

_____

_____

_____

_____

_____

August 1

*T*oday I know that it is just wasting my energy to try to change people, places and things. By looking within, I can discover what really needs to be changed and then turn it over to my Higher Power to be released.

August 2

Today I will take enough time to do something good for myself only. I will buy myself a gift or spend worthwhile time doing something pleasant and fulfilling. I have enough time today and I deserve this time for myself.

August 3

"We have what we seek. It is there all the time, and if we give it time, it will make itself known to us."
Thomas Merton

Today I will slow down and wait for my answers. I will stop rushing and struggling to find them. They will make themselves known when I am ready to hear them. By just knowing they are here and they will appear in their time, I can relax.

August 4

"Try to find your own
God . . . as you understand
Him."

Dr. Bob
Co-founder, AA

In quiet meditation I listen to my own Higher Power today. I connect with my personal spirituality in my own time and place.

_____

_____

_____

_____

_____

_____

_____

August 5

*T*oday I do not need to say the first thing that comes into my head, or react to what others say to me. Today I can practice restraint of tongue and pen . . . think before I speak . . . and say kind things or nothing at all.

_____

_____

_____

_____

_____

_____

_____

August 6

Today I will do all that I am capable of doing at this time in my life to free myself of past mistakes. And then I will let go and live in my now . . . fully enjoying today.

_____

_____

_____

_____

_____

_____

_____

August 7

The peace that I feel in my life is growing richer every day. As I continue to walk on my spiritual path to recovery, letting myself be guided by truth and love, conflict is leaving, making more room for clarity, serenity and usefulness.

August 8

*T*oday I will take the time and quiet I need to find that place of peace and happiness within me. Whatever happens outside of me will never replace that which I can find within me wherever I am.

August 9

*T*oday I know that my Higher Power is guiding me through the changes that I choose to make in my life. I have all the energy that I need today to make these changes as easily and effortlessly as I wish.

August 10

I *will take the time today to stop and give a gift to someone needy, smile at a stranger or help a small child. I will take the time to do at least one thing that I usually find myself too busy to do, and I will inwardly smile at myself, taking the time to experience the feelings of my own kindness.*

August 11

*"So listen to your heart.
That is where your Light
is and your truth."*

*T*oday I am letting go of all judgments. I am
releasing all negative emotions. I am quietly
going within and trusting my inner spirit and
I will know what is right for me.

_____

_____

_____

_____

_____

_____

August 12

Today is a day of opportunities. I am open and ready to find them all, knowing that I am receiving all the guidance I need to move forward and be happy.

_____

_____

_____

_____

_____

_____

_____

August 13

*T*oday I trust what I feel and I listen to my inner voice. It does not matter if it is logical or if others agree. My feelings and emotions guide me on a path that is right for me.

_____

_____

_____

_____

_____

_____

August 14

Today I will spend some time putting my own needs aside to help someone else. It is so good to know that I can be filled with such good feelings and I get so much when I give of myself.

_____

_____

_____

_____

_____

_____

August 15

I decide for myself what I value and what rules I wish to live by today.

living by my own rules

It feels so good to know that I am capable of making my own decisions and following my own path. My Higher Power is my guide, my inner voice, my teacher and my friend.

_____

_____

_____

_____

_____

_____

August 16

*T*oday I know that whatever is in my life, I have put there; therefore, I can let it go as well. Today I have faith and trust that I can take an honest look at what needs to be changed in my life.

_____

_____

_____

_____

_____

_____

August 17

I have all the time in the world to do God's will for me today. I trust that my Higher Powr is filling me with all the energy that I need for this twenty-four hours.

August 18

I value myself today. I value every-thing about me. I am finding people who value me as much as I value myself. I am attracting people who treat me with love and respect.

August 19

*T*oday I am beginning to experience all that I am, a unique and interdependent human being. I feel complete, alive and unlimited. I am free to experiene love and joy.

_____

_____

_____

_____

_____

_____

August 20

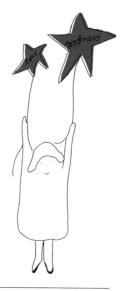

*G*od is guiding me in all my thoughts and plans and actions. I have given up all my struggling and self-defeating messages and have turned over all my thoughts to the power and energy of goodness and love.

_____

_____

_____

_____

_____

_____

August 21

*T*oday I accept all the responsibilities of my life. It feels good to know that I am in charge of my life, that I am at choice in my life and I can accept the outcome of my decisions.

_____

_____

_____

_____

_____

_____

_____

August 22

*E*verywhere I turn I know that I am being supported by powerful, positive energy. I am finding love and support wherever I go.

_____

_____

_____

_____

_____

_____

August 23

"The clearer the path, the easier it is to see the holes in it."

Frank Seymore

I no longer want to repeat the same mistakes over and over again. Today I take the time to slow down and examine the source of my difficulties so that I can move on a clear path with freedom

_____

_____

_____

_____

_____

_____

August 24

I feel 10 feet tall

I am so pleased
with all the
growth that I am
experiencing. It is
okay to feel good
about myself . . .
and I do.

August 25

Today I am open to be touched by love, by joy, by nature. Today I put aside all the happiness that I seek so that I can be free to experience the joy of this very moment . . . right now.

August 26

Today I am discovering who I am. Today I am becoming my person, worthy of developing all of me. Today I am beginning to know that I am okay just the way I am.

August 27

Today I am worthy of being gentle with myself.

I am worthy of it and I am going to give myself gentleness and softness.

I am developing a new habit of being softer with myself today . . . of not driving myself so hard.

I will stop for a moment and get renewed by the energy that I receive when I know that my Higher Power is holding my hand.

August 28

Everywhere I turn I find positive and loving people. My heart is full of peace and love.

_____

_____

_____

_____

_____

_____

August 29

*I*t feels so good to be alive and to be part of this universe. No matter where I am in my life today, no matter what it is that I am doing, I know that I am growing richer and richer with love and with life.

August 30

*T*oday I respect my body, mind and spirit and am taking care of all three. I am gentle and nurturing, putting my needs first. Only then can I be well enough to help others with their needs.

August 31

*T*oday I know I am worthy of having success in my life. I am listening to what I tell myself with gentleness and love, putting a stop to any self-talk that does not make me feel good about myself.

_____

_____

_____

_____

_____

_____

September 1

All my needs are
being met easily
and effortlessly today. I
simply turn them over to
my Higher Power and do
the footwork.

_____

_____

_____

_____

_____

_____

_____

September 2

Today I will experience each moment to the *fullest*. Each moment is unique within itself and the less I carry with me from the previous moment, the freer I am to experience the joy of the now.

_____

_____

_____

_____

_____

_____

September 3

I have all the strength that I need today to accept the realities of my life. I am guided on a path of learning and growth and healing.

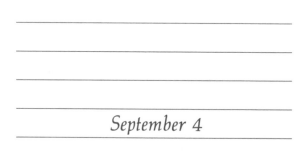

September 4

I am a terrific human being! I deserve wonderful things to happen to me . . . and they are.

_____

_____

_____

_____

_____

_____

September 5

*T*oday I am listening to my self-talk with a gentle, nonjudgmental ear. It is okay to make mistakes today. I am giving myself positive messages with permission to accept both my victories and defeats.

September 6

Today I am getting all the guidance I need to take care of myself. I need not keep pushing beyond my limitations. I am learning to listen to my body and my mind and rest when I get the message.

September 7

THIS moment

I am exactly where I am supposed to be today. Everything about this day, this place, this moment is perfect. Everything about me is perfect in this moment.

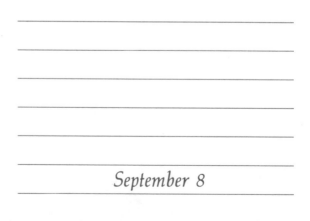

September 8

It feels so comforting when I trust my own truth. It is both powerful and peaceful to know that we are all at choice. Each and every one of us is being led on a path to peace and love.

September 9

*Peace is flowing
through me every-
where today, pouring
all over my mind and
my body . . . releasing
all my tensions and
anxiety . . . emptying
me of all my negativity
and fear. I am being
filled with peace and
love and serenity.*

September 10

I am letting go of all that is holding me back from spiritual progress today. My path is becoming easier and easier as I open myself to faith and trust.

_____

_____

_____

_____

_____

_____

September 11

*E*ach step I take today
makes me feel better
and better.

Today I know I have all
that I need to do exactly
what must be done and
go exactly where I need
to go.

_____

_____

_____

_____

_____

_____

September 12

Today I am taking all the steps that I can for my recovery. My Higher Power is giving me all the guidance I need and I am full of joy and gratitude that I am growing and healing today.

_____

_____

_____

_____

_____

_____

September 13

I am so grateful for the guidance I am receiving in my recovery. The more I open myself up to admitting I can't do it alone, the more I realize help is always there.

September 14

my parents

Today I am willing to take responsibility for my own life. I am willing to grow up and let go of my parents. I am filled with a sense of my own power and I choose not to give it away.

_____

_____

_____

_____

_____

_____

September 15

*L*ight is shining on my path today as I face in the direction of love and goodness. One step at a time it is leading me exactly where I need to be.

_____

_____

_____

_____

_____

_____

_____

September 16

Today I continue to seek and find people who are positive, healthy and nurturing.

September 17

> "You must lose a fly to
> catch a trout."
> George Herbert

I f something isn't working for me today, I am willing to let go of the struggle. I trust that God has something better in store for me.

September 18

I grow and learn from everything that happens. Today I am keeping my eyes open and my head clear so that I don't have to make the same mistake twice.

_____

_____

_____

_____

_____

_____

_____

September 19

I am very grateful for this day. I am grateful for all the love and the inspiration that I receive from my Higher Power whenever I ask. I just stop and tune in to this universal energy and am transformed to the level of my willingness.

_____

_____

_____

_____

_____

_____

_____

September 20

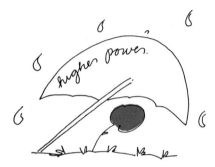

*T*oday I am taking whatever comes in my stride. Today I know that I can handle any change, any surprise, anything at all as long as I remember that my Higher Power is with me and that I am never alone.

_____

_____

_____

_____

_____

_____

_____

September 21

*T*oday I will find someone who needs my love. Today I will share my strength, hope and experience so that someone else can be reborn.

_____

_____

_____

_____

_____

_____

September 22

*T*oday I am really listening to the messages that I tell myself. Today I want to feel good. Today I am changing all my negative messages to positive ones.

_____

_____

_____

_____

_____

_____

_____

September 23

*T*oday I choose to do things for me that make me feel good about myself. Today is a perfect day to do something that I have been putting off.

_____

_____

_____

_____

_____

_____

_____

September 24

*T*oday I am looking within to discover what I am holding on to from the past. Today I am willing to let go of all old anger and resentments that keep me stuck in tension and pain.

_____

_____

_____

_____

_____

_____

_____

September 25

*T*oday I have all the courage I need to take the step forward in my life that I have been putting off. I can manage one step at a time, one change at a time, with ease and with confidence.

September 26

". . . We are going to know a new freedom and a new happiness."

The Promises
Big Book

Freedom and happiness are not goals. They are by-products of a way of life that demands rigorous honesty and the willingness to grow along spiritual lines. Once the choice is made to live according to our truth, the path that follows seems so logical as to make us wonder why we took so long to decide to walk it.

Today I am living according to my truth, knowing that freedom and happiness are the result.

September 27

I am learning to trust my intuition and I am willing to act on this inner guidance. I am taking positive and healthy actions today and my life is getting better and better.

_____

_____

_____

_____

_____

_____

September 28

I love myself and all that I am today. My fears are just one part of all that I am. I am a human being on a progressive path to recovery and every part of me is important in the making up of who I am.

September 29

I am one of the miracles of this universe and I am connected to everything that was ever created. I can pick up the phone or sit in quiet meditation, choosing to make contact with a friend or with my Higher Power, or with both. Today I know that I am never alone.

_____

_____

_____

_____

_____

_____

September 30

I am grateful for the power I have over the future of my life. I am being guided at all times to use my power with wisdom and love.

_____

_____

_____

_____

_____

_____

October 1

*A*s I am learning to see the world through the eyes of love and compassion, I am becoming more and more full of love and compassion for myself and others. I deserve to feel good about myself today and I am learning how.

October 2

I choose to be in places and situations and with people where I feel good about myself. I deserve to feel good and I trust that my heart will tell me where to go.

good people

good places

October 3

just wait

*T*oday I can wait until all negative and hostile feelings lose their power over me before I say or do anything. I can take the time to breathe in peace and love, no matter what is going on in my life.

_____

_____

_____

_____

_____

_____

October 4

*T*oday I am developing a world of peace for myself both inside and out. Today I know that I am always only one breath away from peace, one prayer away from serenity.

_____

_____

_____

_____

_____

_____

_____

October 5

*T*oday I am doing everything I can to totally accept me as I am. Today I am doing everything that I can to totally accept you as you are. I am free to have an honest relationship with me and you today.

October 6

I no longer decide what I should feel. That is very limiting. If I limit my negative feelings, I limit my positive feelings as well. Today I am opening myself to all feelings. That gives me great joy.

_____

_____

_____

_____

_____

_____

October 7

*T*oday I am stretching myself and taking new risks. Today faith is working to replace the fear that has held me back.

_____

_____

_____

_____

_____

_____

_____

October 8

a lesson to growth

Today I am learning to trust that no matter what is going on in my life I am in the process of growth.

_____

_____

_____

_____

_____

_____

_____

October 9

*T*oday I will do something very special just for me. I will treat myself to something I want to have or do and feel good about myself while I do it. My life is very important to me and I have the right to be happy.

_____

_____

_____

_____

_____

_____

_____

October 10

FirST others

*T*oday I know it is okay to place myself first sometimes. Today I am doing something very special for myself.

_____

_____

_____

_____

_____

_____

_____

October 11

I do not let pain or discomfort stop me from looking at myself in a true and honest light. I do not run away from myself to-day or block or disguise my reality. I face my life fully today to learn from its lessons.

October 12

"Serenity is not the absence of pain. Serenity is reaching beyond surface appearances into inner truth, knowing God is working for our highest good."
Sandy Scotto Siraco

I am at peace today knowing that God is doing for me what I cannot do for myself.

October 13

I can accept whatever I am feeling today. Without resistance my feelings pass and I am then open to experience whatever is next.

October 14

I have a quiet place within me where I can rest today. I have a quiet place that I can go to that offers peace, comfort and healing. It is as close as this moment . . . as close as a breath. This place is mine whenever I want it.

_____

_____

_____

_____

_____

_____

October 15

... just live today!

T*oday I know that I have done the best I can with my life. Today I know that I am at choice and what I choose right now creates new memories. Today I choose to continue to do the very best.*

October 16

The world would sleep if things were run by (people) who say, "It can't be done!"
Philander Johnson
(amended)

*T*oday I look at my Higher Power for strength, courage and direction. I gather my own strength and confidence from all positive resources and follow my own inner voice.

_____

_____

_____

_____

_____

_____

_____

October 17

I am full of joy in the discovery that I am okay just the way I am. Today I can accept all of me and that is a miracle.

October 18

I am so grateful that I
have a power greater
than myself to turn to
when I do not have the
answers. I am so grateful
for the program of recov-
ery that has brought me
joy and purpose and love.

October 19

It feels so good to know that I am healing from my old wounds. As I bring love and acceptance to myself today, I can watch the pain disappear and I feel so much better about myself.

October 20

Today I know that I am not alone. Today I know that God guides me in all situations and all I have to do to get help is to ask for it.

_____

_____

_____

_____

_____

_____

_____

October 21

*T*oday I pray for the knowledge of God's will for me and the power to carry it through.

_____

_____

_____

_____

_____

_____

_____

October 22

*G*od is guiding me with every step and every breath I take today. All I have to do is wake up, ask for help, guidance and knowledge to a power greater than myself, and trust that I will know what to do.

_____

_____

_____

_____

_____

_____

_____

October 23

*T*oday I find healthy ways to express my anger and resentments so that I can be free of them. Today I empty myself of all anger and resentments so that I can let love come into my heart.

October 24

*N*o matter how busy I think I am, I will share a part of me with someone else today. I am discovering the joy of giving and I will take the time to stop and share a part of me.

_____

_____

_____

_____

_____

_____

October 25

I am learning to trust the positive and loving people in my life today.

October 26

negative
feelings

Today I practice restraint of tongue and pen and I do not hurt anyone intentionally. Today I give myself time to express myself appropriately. Today I go beyond negative feelings. I act as if I am coming from a place of love.

October 27

It feels so good to like all of me today. I feel warm and comforted in knowing that I am just fine . . . just the way I am.

October 28

I am becoming open to loving others and letting myself feel the love that other people have for me today.

_____

_____

_____

_____

_____

_____

October 29

Today my happiness radiates from within me.

Gary Seidler

October 30

Today I am aware of all those who have helped in my life. My heart is filled with gratitude and love. I know that I am not alone.

October 31

GOODNESS AND LOVE

*I*t feels so wonderful to know that I am truly full of goodness and love and that I can begin from this very moment to choose to express that part of myself.

_____

_____

_____

_____

_____

_____

November 1

I am filled with all the strength and energy I need today to follow my own truth. I am willing to take risks today and find out for myself what works for me in my life.

November 2

silence

*I*n the silence of my meditation, I receive
guidance and direction. I am filled with all
the power I need to take my next step.

_____

_____

_____

_____

_____

_____

November 3

I speak from my own truth today. I come from a place of love or I say nothing at all.

November 4

*T*oday I am doing everything that I can to be in the now. That means letting go all the baggage of the past that I am still carrying with me.

_____

_____

_____

_____

_____

_____

November 5

Today I know that I am in charge of the quality of my life. I am growing in the ability to become aware of the thoughts that have been controlling me.

November 6

*T*oday I fight for what is really important to
me in a spiritual way. I no longer waste my
good energy fighting to win or to be right.

_____

_____

_____

_____

_____

_____

_____

November 7

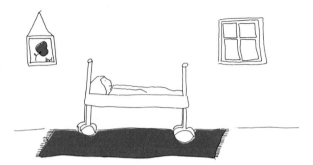

When I get up today, no matter how I feel, I begin my day by letting it go to a power greater than myself. I am beginning this day by giving myself the gift of prayer and meditation.

_____

_____

_____

_____

_____

_____

November 8

FULLY OPEN!

Today I am fully alive, fully open to feel all
that there is . . . knowing that I can
handle all that comes my way.

_____

_____

_____

_____

_____

_____

November 9

*"God grant me the serenity
to accept the things I cannot change,
The courage to change the things I can
And the wisdom to know the difference.
Thy will, not mine, be done."*

*I*n moments of stress, doubt, uncertainty,
anger or pain, I can pause and say the
serenity prayer, knowing that I will get all the
strength, courage and wisdom that I need.

_____

_____

_____

_____

_____

_____

November 10

TODAY!

*T*oday I am taking the time I need to look at my growth and progress. I celebrate being alive. I celebrate the good in me. Today I celebrate me.

_____

_____

_____

_____

_____

_____

November 11

When I find my now full of yesterday's feelings, I can ask for God to remove them. I can pray to turn them over to a power greater than myself, so that they will lose their power for me. I no longer need to hold on to memories which create feelings that make me upset or unhappy.

November 12

*T*oday I am looking within to discover what I am holding on to from the past. Today I am willing to let go of all old anger and resentments that keep me stuck in tension and pain.

_____

_____

_____

_____

_____

_____

November 13

*T*oday I know that whatever ability, talents and energy I have are perfect for this moment. Today I know that God gives me all that I need to do what he wants me to do in this day.

_____

_____

_____

_____

_____

_____

November 14

Today I am learning to think and act in a positive way that is healthy for my mind, body and spirit.

_____

_____

_____

_____

_____

_____

_____

November 15

Today I know that it does not matter if I cannot see the end of the road. I have absolute faith and trust that I am walking in the right direction and that I am being guided along the way.

November 16

Today I am doing the best that I can with the guidance that I get. I leave the results to my Higher Power and trust that they are for the greatest good.

_____

_____

_____

_____

_____

_____

_____

November 17

*T*oday I can handle whatever comes up, knowing that I am surrounded with all the positive energies of good and love in the universe.

_____

_____

_____

_____

_____

_____

November 18

I am so full of love and
joy today. *I* see it
everywhere I look, and
feel it with every breath
that I take.

_____

_____

_____

_____

_____

_____

November 19

Today I am following my own inner guide, knowing that I am coming from the best of who I am. That makes me feel good about me. That gives me great pleasure.

_____

_____

_____

_____

_____

_____

November 20

I trust God's plan for me today. I know that I am being guided at all times.

I know all I need to know in any given minute.

November 21

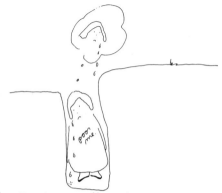

*T*oday I refuse to allow the magnetic tape of self-pity to trap me. Today I avoid negative thinking and replace it as soon as I notice it is part of me.

_____

_____

_____

_____

_____

_____

_____

November 22

> "I am as my Creator made me, and since He is satisfied, so am I."
>
> Minnie Smith

*I*t feels so good to like myself today. It feels so good to accept myself today. It feels so good to know that I am exactly where I need to be, doing what is right for me in this day.

_____

_____

_____

_____

_____

_____

November 23

*I*mmediately release everything that I am struggling with today. I release everything to my Higher Power, knowing that I am getting all the help I need today.

November 24

...early limitations...

Today I celebrate all of me exactly as I am.

_____

_____

_____

_____

_____

_____

November 25

Today I am willing to let go of all the old ways which keep me from growing on a spiritual path. Today I am willing to push aside all the blocks that stand between me and love.

_____

_____

_____

_____

_____

_____

_____

November 26

Today I choose to stay in the reality of my life and feel all there is to feel. Today I am willing to feel the pain so that I can feel the joy.

November 27

I know today that I am nothing alone. I am willing to let go of any struggle that keeps me on a path of doing things my way. I know that all I have to do is ask for help and it is there for me!

November 28

I am very grateful for the gift of this day. It is mine to do exactly what I choose and I choose to use it for good and love.

November 29

my truth

Today I know my journey to peace and serenity begins with me. Today I have the faith and trust to seek my answers from within.

_____

_____

_____

_____

_____

_____

November 30

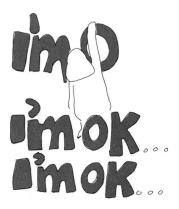

i'm ok... i'm ok...

I feel okay about me today and that is terrific.

_____

_____

_____

_____

_____

_____

_____

December 1

*T*oday I have a "gratitude" attitude.

_____

_____

_____

_____

_____

_____

December 2

I am beginning to trust myself today. There is a place deep within me that tells me I am okay and guides me along my path in recovery.

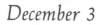

December 3

I am getting to know myself today. I accept who I am today. I like myself today.

_____

_____

_____

_____

_____

_____

December 4

*T*oday is full of miracles.

December 5

I feel lighter and better about myself when I don't procrastinate. Today I am discovering the freedom in completing at least one thing that I have put off.

December 6

Today I know that I can get through anything that happens in this day with the help of my Higher Power.

_____

_____

_____

_____

_____

_____

_____

December 7

It feels so good to accept myself just as I am today. All my thoughts and actions and emotions are right where they belong.

_____

_____

_____

_____

_____

_____

_____

December 8

I have a right to have my needs met. In order to have them met, I am expressing them to the people who can help me today.

_____

_____

_____

_____

_____

_____

_____

_____

December 9

*T*oday I trust the positive and loving people to whom I am attracted. Today I am free to share from my heart, knowing that what I say will be treated with love and respect.

_____

_____

_____

_____

_____

_____

_____

December 10

The world cannot change overnight, nor can I. Just one step at a time, one day at a time, I am exactly where I need to be to get to exactly where I am going. I trust this process today.

December 11

There is something special waiting for me to do with this day. I know that when it is time, I will be inspired from a place deep within myself. I trust that I will know what to do when the time is right.

December 12

my old
burdens

*T*oday I am willing to begin to share all of
me with another human being. I am
willing to trust that this process will free me
from the burdens of my past. I am ready to let
go.

_____

_____

_____

_____

_____

_____

_____

December 13

*T*oday I can look back with love in my heart, knowing that every moment, every experience of my life has been necessary, valuable and significant.

December 14

Today I am experiencing all of my life. It is exciting to be alive in each moment.

December 15

Whatever I am thinking right now is creating how I am feeling. I turn to positive and loving thoughts because I choose to feel good.

December 16

When I have done all the foot-work I know to do and things are still not working out, I know today that it is time to meditate. I have faith that my answer is still to come.

have faith

_____

_____

_____

_____

_____

_____

_____

December 17

*T*oday I welcome all my feelings. Today I deserve to feel joy and love and gratitude and warmth and affection, just to name a few!

December 18

In quiet and meditation I find emotional balance. I feel myself growing closer and closer to my Higher Power and I find love.

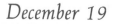

December 19

*T*oday I know that I am powerless over all the addictions, obsessions, compulsions and dependencies in my life. Today I am willing to let them go to a power greater than myself.

power greater than myself

December 20

*T*oday I seek spiritual understanding beyond everything else. I choose peace and love and joy as my goals.

_____

_____

_____

_____

_____

_____

_____

December 21

I can handle anything that comes up today . . . even if it is only for a moment at a time.

December 22

*A*s I start this day with quiet meditation, I feel myself becoming still and at peace. At any time during the day I can bring my mind back to this moment.

_____
_____
_____
_____
_____
_____
_____

December 23

*T*oday I am learn-
ing to be increas-
ingly aware of my
spiritual life.

_____

_____

_____

_____

_____

_____

December 24

*L*ove fills me and heals me as I open to connect with the people that God has placed in my life.

_____

_____

_____

_____

_____

_____

December 25

I live today as I want to remember my life.

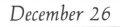

_____
_____
_____
_____
_____
_____
_____

December 26

*T*oday I am unveiling all my layers of self-doubt and letting them go. Today I am taking back all the power that I have given to others by discovering the courage that comes from my own wisdom.

December 27

Today I am slowing down my pace. I do not have to accomplish the entire world in this day. It is one day. Today I have time to stop and smell the flowers.

_____

_____

_____

_____

_____

_____

December 28

Through prayer and meditation, God guides me to the appropriate people for direction in the important decisions I must make in my life. I trust my answers to be there when the time is right.

_____

_____

_____

_____

_____

_____

_____

December 29

It feels so good to help other people and to know that I have something to give them. It feels so good to have turned my own life around so that it can benefit others.

_____

_____

_____

_____

_____

_____

_____

December 30

*T*oday I know that I am at choice. Today I have all the willingness . . . all the energy and all the guidance I need to continue to choose the path of peace and love and joy.

_____

_____

_____

_____

_____

_____

December 31

Other Books By Ruth Fishel

Time For Joy: Daily Affirmations

In this book, delightfully illustrated by Bonny Lowell, Ruth Fishel takes the reader through a calendar year with quotations, thoughts and healing energizing affirmations.

ISBN 0-932194-82-6   **(Soft cover 4x6 375 pp.)**
Code 4826 .... **$6.95**

The Journey Within: A Spiritual Path to Recovery

This book will lead you from your dysfunction to the place within where your wounded being can grow healthy and strong, the place where miracles happen.

ISBN 0-932194-41-9   **(Soft cover 5½x8½ 192 pg.)**
Code 4419 .... **$8.95**

**Learning To Live In The Now:
6-Week Personal Plan to Recovery**

Enjoy today without worry for the future or regret for the past. There is only this moment. Enjoy it with this loving book.

ISBN 0-932194-62-1   **(Soft cover 6x9 160 pg.)**
Code 4621 .... **$8.95**

Shipping and handling: All orders shipped UPS unless weight exceeds 200 lbs., special routing is requested or delivery territory is outside continental U.S. Orders outside United States shipped either Air Parcel Post or Surface Parcel Post. Shipping and handling charges apply to all orders shipped whether UPS, Book Rate, Library Rate, Air or Surface Parcel Post or Common Carrier and will be charged as follows. Orders less than $25.00 in value add $2.00 minimum. Orders from $25.00 to $50.00 in value (after discount) add $2.50 minimum. Orders greater than $50.00 in value (after discount) add 6% of value. Orders greater than $25.00 outside United States add 15% of value. We are not responsible for loss or damage unless material is shipped UPS. Allow 3-5 weeks after receipt of order for delivery. Prices are subject to change without prior notice.

Health Communications, Inc.
Enterprise Center, 3201 S.W. 15th Street
Deerfield Beach, FL 33442   1-800-851-9100